The Strange Shoe

Retold by Beverley Randell
Illustrated by Pat Reynolds

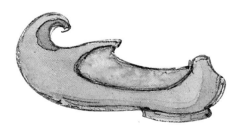

Once upon a time, some animals lived in a green Asian jungle, far, far away from the world of people. None of them had ever seen a man or a woman or a child.

One day, a large black bear came lumbering along a jungle path. She stopped when she saw something strange lying in a clearing. The black bear had no idea what it was.

It was a man's shoe, but how it came to be in the jungle was a mystery.

3

The bear had never seen anything like a shoe before. She walked all around it and sniffed at it with her long nose.

"It smells strange," she said. "It must be the tough skin of some fruit that I don't know about. It has turned brown, like an old banana skin."

While the bear was still smelling the shoe, a handsome tiger came prowling out of the long grass and stopped to look.

The bear pushed the shoe toward the tiger. "This old brown skin smells strange," she said, "and I don't know what fruit it is. Can you tell me?"

The tiger rolled the shoe over with his paws and he sniffed at it, too. "I agree it smells odd," he said, "but it is nothing like a fruit. It smells too salty to be a fruit. I think it's a dried-up fish. Take a look at its shape!"

The bear rolled the shoe over again. Although it did look rather like a fish, she still thought it was a thick piece of skin that had once been part of a strange fruit. "It's not a fish," she told the tiger. "It has no fins and no scales. It must be a sort of banana skin."

An inquisitive monkey, who had been leaping around on the branches above the bear and the tiger, dropped down into the clearing. He scampered over to look at the shoe.

"Let me see," he said. "No — you are both wrong. I eat a lot of nuts, and I can tell a nutshell when I see one." He reached out and snatched the shoe with his long arm. "Anyway, this nutshell is too old to bother about," he said. "The nut that used to fit inside it has gone."

"It's not a nutshell," said the bear. "It's a skin that once belonged to a fruit."

"It can't be a skin from a fruit, and it can't be a nutshell," said the tiger. "It's definitely a dried-up fish."

Then a graceful spotted deer stepped into the clearing and prodded at the shoe with her hard hoof.

"You are all wrong," she said. "This thing is a piece of bark that has fallen from a tree."

But the bear, the tiger, and the monkey did not agree. "It's not a piece of bark," they all said together, and they went on arguing in loud voices.

The noise they made brought a lean wolf to the clearing. He trotted over to look at the shoe.

"I know what that is," he said. "It's a bird's nest. Look, the eggs would have fit at this end, where there was room for the mother bird to sit." The wolf licked his muzzle as he remembered how much he enjoyed a mouthful of eggs. Then he sniffed at the shoe. "But one of the eggs must have broken and gone bad. That's why it smells strange."

"It's not a bird's nest," shouted all the other animals.

"It's a fruit," growled the bear.

"It's a fish," roared the tiger.

"It's a nutshell," screeched the monkey.

"It's a piece of bark," snorted the deer.

And the wolf put his head in the air and howled, "It's a bird's nest. I'm sure it is."

13

"What a hullabaloo! You have woken me up with your hullabaloo," hooted a tawny owl, as she climbed out of a hole in a tree. "Let me see this thing that you are arguing about so loudly. I may be able to tell you what it is."

And she flew down to look at the shoe.

"Aha!" she said. "Sometimes I fly far from the jungle and see strange things in distant places. Yes. I have seen one of these before. It is not a fruit. Nor is it a fish or a nut or a piece of bark or a bird's nest. It's a man's shoe."

"A shoe?" cried all the animals. "What is a shoe? What is a man?"

"You ask, *What is a man?*" said the tawny owl. "A man is a strange animal who stands on two legs just as I do. But he is not a bird. He cannot fly, and he has no feathers. He has to make his own."

"Make his own feathers!" exclaimed the bear. "That is ridiculous. You must be joking."

"I'm not joking," said the owl. "Men **do** make their own feathers. And because their skin is thin and soft, their feet are easily hurt. Men make these things called *shoes* to put on their feet. Shoes stop their soft feet from getting hurt."

"Soft feet!" said the deer, who had very hard hoofs. "That can't be true. No one in the world could walk on **soft** feet. The idea is absurd."

"Make things? Put them on?" scoffed the tiger. "Animals do not put things on their feet!" And he roared with laughter.

"Men **can** make things. They make many things," said the owl. "They can even make fire. Men are clever and dangerous animals. Believe me!"

But the jungle animals would not believe anything the owl said. They became angry.

"Animals with sore feet and no feathers can't be dangerous," roared the tiger.

"You must be crazy," growled the bear.

"You have just made up a silly story," snorted the deer.

"You are not telling the truth," screeched the monkey. "Whatever that thing is, it is not a *man's shoe.*"

"We don't want someone like you living with us in our beautiful green jungle," howled the wolf. "As you won't tell the truth, you had better get out. Go-o-o! Go-o-o!"

Then all the animals turned on the owl. They roared and growled and screeched and howled and chased her through the trees.

"I **am** telling the truth," cried the owl, as she flew away to a distant part of the jungle, where she could live in peace.

"It's true. It's a shoe! It's true. It's a shoe!" she hooted.

"Tu-whit, tu-whoo. Tu-whit, tu-whoo."

Of course, the owl was right, absolutely right, even though no one believed her... and one day the animals would find out just how right she was.

But that is another story.

A play
The Strange Shoe

People in the play

Narrator

Monkey

Bear

Deer

Tiger

Wolf

Owl

Scene — A jungle clearing

Narrator

Once upon a time, some animals lived in a green Asian jungle, far, far away from the world of people. None of them had ever seen a man or a woman or a child. So when they saw something strange lying in a clearing in the jungle, none of them knew that it was a man's shoe. The first animal to walk into the clearing was a large black bear.

Bear (sniffing at the shoe)

I've never seen anything like this before! It smells strange. It must be the tough skin of some fruit that I don't know about. It has turned brown, like an old banana skin.

Narrator

Then a handsome tiger came prowling out of the long grass and stopped to look.

Bear (pushing the shoe toward the tiger)

This old brown skin smells strange, and I don't know what fruit it is. Can you tell me?

Tiger (rolling the shoe over and sniffing it)

I agree it smells odd, but it is nothing like a fruit. It smells too salty to be a fruit. I think it's a dried-up fish. Take a look at its shape!

Bear (taking the shoe back)

It does look rather like a fish, but it's not a fish, because it has no fins and no scales. It must be a sort of banana skin.

Narrator

An inquisitive monkey dropped down from the branches and scampered over to look.

Monkey

Let me see. No — you are both wrong. I eat a lot of nuts, and I can tell a nutshell when I see one.

Bear and Tiger (both together)

It's not a nutshell!

Monkey (picking up the shoe)

Anyway, this nutshell is too old to bother about. The nut that used to fit inside it has gone. There's nothing left to eat.

Bear

It's not a nutshell. It's a skin that once belonged to a fruit.

Tiger

It can't be a skin from a fruit, and it can't be a nutshell. It's definitely a dried-up fish.

Narrator

Then a spotted deer stepped into the clearing.

Deer (prodding the shoe with her hoof)

I've been listening, and I have to say that you are all wrong. This thing is a piece of bark that has fallen from a tree.

Bear, Tiger, and Monkey (all together)

It's not a piece of bark!

Narrator

A lean wolf heard all the noise and trotted into the clearing to look at the shoe.

Wolf

I know what it is. It's a bird's nest. Look, the eggs would have fit at this end, where there was room for the mother bird to sit. But one of the eggs must have broken and gone bad. That's why it smells strange.

Bear, Tiger, Monkey, and Deer (loudly)

It's not a bird's nest. It's not!

Bear (growling)

It's a fruit.

Tiger (roaring)

It's a fish.

Monkey (screeching)

It's a nutshell.

Deer

It's a piece of bark.

Wolf (howling)

Oo-oo-oo! Oo-oo-oo!

It's a bird's nest. I'm sure it is.

Narrator

The noise the animals made woke a tawny owl, who had been sleeping in a hole in a tree. She hooted as she climbed out.

Owl

Tu-whit, tu-whoo! Tu-whit, tu-whoo! What a hullabaloo! You have woken me up with your hullabaloo. Let me see this thing that you are arguing about so loudly. I may be able to tell you what it is.

Narrator

So the owl flew down to look at the shoe.

Owl

Aha! Sometimes I fly far from the jungle and see strange things in distant places. Yes, I have seen one of these before. It is not a fruit. Nor is it a fish or a nut or a piece of bark or a bird's nest. It's a man's shoe.

Wolf

A shoe? What is a *shoe*? And what is a *man*?

Owl

You ask, *What is a man?* A man is a strange animal who stands on two legs, just as I do. But he is not a bird. He can't fly, and he has no feathers. He has to make his own.

Bear

Make his own feathers! That's ridiculous. You must be joking.

Owl

I'm not joking. Men **do** make their own feathers. And because their skin is thin and soft, their feet are easily hurt. Men make these things called *shoes* to put on their feet. Shoes stop their soft feet from getting hurt.

Deer

Soft feet! That can't be true. My feet aren't soft. I have very hard hoofs. No one in the world could walk on **soft** feet. The idea is absurd.

Tiger (roaring with laughter)

Animals don't put things on their feet!

Owl

Men do make shoes to put on their feet, whatever you think.

Monkey

Men can't make things. No animals make things. Animals just find things.

Owl

Men can make things! They make many things. They can even make fire. Men are clever and dangerous animals. Believe me!

Tiger

Animals with only two legs, sore feet, and no feathers can't be dangerous.

Bear

You must be crazy!

Deer

You have just made up a silly story.

Monkey

You are not telling the truth. Whatever that thing is, it is not a *man's shoe!*

Wolf

We don't want someone like you living with us in our beautiful green jungle. As you won't tell the truth, you had better get out.

Tiger (roaring)

Be off with you!

Bear (growling)

Yes — be off with you!

Monkey (screeching)

You had better go **now**.

Deer

Go — or we shall have to make you!

Wolf (howling)

Go-o-o! Go-o-o!

Narrator

Then all the animals turned on the owl. They roared and growled and screeched and howled and chased her through the trees.

Owl (flying ahead of them and hooting)

Well, I don't want to stay with you! I'm going to fly away to a distant part of the jungle, where I can live in peace. I **am** telling the truth, whatever you say.

Narrator

The owl flew away, leaving all the other animals behind her.

Owl

It's true! It's a shoe!
It's true! It's a shoe!
Tu-whit, tu-whoo!
Tu-whit, tu-whoo!

Narrator

Of course the owl was right, absolutely right, even though no one believed her... and one day the animals would find out just how right she was.

But that is another story.